MW01235644

Bankers, Mustangs, and Marsh Tackies

By

Donna Campbell Smith

Old Gray Mare Press

Published by Old Gray Mare Press
PO Box 351
Franklinton, NC 27525

Bankers, Mustangs and Marsh Tackies

First Edition

Cover art *Fighting Stallions* by M. Theresa Brown

ISBN-13:
978-0692651636 (Old Gray Mare Press)

ISBN-10:
0692651632

Dedication

To the wild horses of the Carolina Coast and the people who have worked selflessly to save them.

Contents

Chapter One
Where Did They Come From?

North Carolina's Outer Banks are home to several herds of wild horses. They have roamed the beaches and maritime forests of these barrier islands for over 400 years. In the 1950s they numbered over 5,000. Today there are only a few hundred left, and people worry that the horses will eventually be crowded out entirely.

Considering the environment of the islands, one can only marvel that these animals have survived at all. The Outer Banks is a place of fierce hurricanes, scorching summer heat, and stormy, cold winters. But these little horses are hardy. They graze on tough sea grasses and drink brackish water that wells up into holes they dig in the sand with their hooves.

Scientists believe horses roamed North America as long as 58 million years ago, but when Columbus arrived in America in 1492 he found no horses. They seem to have suddenly disappeared a few thousand years before Columbus' arrival. It is thought that some contagious disease might have wiped them out. Others think the prehistoric horses failed to adapt to the climatic changes that took place at the time, or possibly they did not have enough food.

In any case, in the 1500's when Spanish explorers came to the New World searching for gold, they reintroduced the horse to America. History tells us Columbus brought Spanish horses to the West Indies and established ranches in Hispaniola (now the Dominican Republic). By the year 1500, ranches in the West Indies were selling horses and livestock to voyagers who stopped there to replenish their supplies.

When the Spaniards arrived on the coast of North American, they brought cattle and swine to use for food and horses to use for transportation over land. In some cases ships wrecked off North Carolina's dangerous coastline and horses swam ashore, free to run wild on the islands. Often the horses were considered disposable to the explorers. They were purchased in route, used in mainland exploration, and left behind when the explorers sailed home.

Explorer, Luis Vasquez de Ayllon, sent three expeditions to the Carolina coast from Toledo, Spain. In 1526 he even attempted to establish a colony. Ship's records show he brought five hundred men, women, children and slaves. In addition, he brought ninety horses that he had purchased from the Hispaniola ranches. The colony failed when Ayllon and many of the colonists died of yellow fever. The survivors returned to Hispaniola, leaving the horses behind.

Many documented reports support the theory that Spanish horses were brought to North Carolina long before any colonies were established.

When the explorers worked their way up the coast from Florida, they found the Carolina coast very interesting. They heard rumors that gold could be found far inland in the mountains. Their sturdy Spanish horses carried them through swamps and forests in their explorations. They did not find gold. The Spanish sailed away, leaving their horses behind. The horses, descendants of the Arabian

3

desert, adapted well to their new home. They flourished and roamed freely for several decades, until the English explorers came onto the scene.

We don't have many written records of how the native people interacted with the horses. We might suppose they used them as a food source. On the other hand, the native people obviously observed the Spaniards riding horses or using them as beasts of burden. It seems likely they might have made similar use of these foreign creatures. One written account of the relationship between horse and native people sounds more like that of a pet.

In *A New Voyage to Carolina* (published in 1709) English explorer, John Lawson reported that the Indians fed the horses corn until they were fat and treated them like pets, not making any other use of them, except to occasionally haul home a deer carcass after a hunt.

The wild horses of the Outer Banks share the same physical characteristics as the Spanish Mustang. They are small and compactly built, standing from 14 to 15.2 hands tall and weighing 800 to 1,000 pounds. They have broad foreheads with a straight or sometimes convex profile and long, silky manes and tails. They have short backs and strong hindquarters with high to medium low tail sets.

Living in harmony with human and wildlife, the horses have played an important role in North Carolina's history, as horses have in all parts of the United States. The horses on the Carolina coast provided horsepower to haul in fishing nets, aided in lifesaving operations, and provided over-land transportation until the automobile's arrival.

According to the December 1933 issue of *National Geographic,* a midwife named Mis' Bashi had a pony named Napoleon who carried her in a two-wheel cart through woods, sand and water to deliver her patients' babies. That same article has a picture of a pony and cart carrying home goods from the steamboat, Missouri. In those days, not much of anything was done without the help of a "sand pony," as the horses were called.

Interest in proving the little horses' heritage developed in the 1980s, along with a burst of development on the Outer Banks. Hotels, condos and shopping centers sprouted up around the small fishing villages, and the future existence of the horses became threatened. Disease plagued the largest herd which lives on Shackleford Banks and the Cedar Island group. Starvation almost wiped out the herd on Carrot Island, and the Corolla herd was cut in half when horses were hit by cars speeding along the newly paved Highway 12.

People living on the islands, as well as tourists who visited the resort area on vacations, loved seeing the horses grazing among the sand dunes and galloping in the surf. They became determined to make sure these beautiful animals would still be around for their grandchildren to enjoy. Protection groups formed, local and federal governments passed protection laws, and the news spread that wild horses in North Carolina were becoming endangered. The people went to work to save the animals that helped build the rich heritage of the Carolinas.

I have enjoyed learning how these horses, once known as Banker Ponies, were an important part of our heritage. Many of the following stories I first wrote for the children's horse magazine, *Young Rider*. I have coupled them in this book with chapters on the historical background that inspired the stories.

Chapter Two
Bess and Betsy of Currituck Banks

People living on the Outer Banks love to tell stories about the wild horses and how they fit into the history of the area. One tale that has been told and retold since the American Revolution is that of a teenage girl and her Banker pony, Black Bess. Betsy Dowdy was the Paul Revere of North Carolina. She is famous for riding Black Bess from her home on the coast, swimming across the Currituck Sound, and galloping inland over fifty miles to Perquimans County to warn that the British were coming. Paul Revere's ride was only sixteen miles over land.

The story begins when the Earl of Dunmore marched his troops south from Virginia to invade Northeastern North Carolina. In November of 1775, Dunmore captured Portsmouth, Virginia. He went on to take over Norfolk. The British wanted control of the harbors to stop the colonies from selling their goods.

It was a tense time in the American Revolution. Up until this point North Carolinians didn't think much about the argument over taxes between the colonies and Britain. But Dunmore's actions were bringing the war close to home. He next traveled south where he barricaded Great Bridge on the Carolina side. In addition to burning homes, Dunmore's men slaughtered the colonists' livestock and horses.

Trade goods were transported from the Carolinas through Great Bridge and to Norfolk for export. Dunmore built a stockade and dismantled part of the bridge, then installed cannons. North Carolina's means of trade and livelihood were now cut off.

On the night of December 6, 1775, the news of Dunmore's capture of Great Bridge reached the Dowdy family who lived on isolated Currituck Banks. A neighbor, Sam Jarvis, brought back a full report after a visit to the mainland. Betsy overheard the story in all its awful details as it was being related to her father. She was further horrified to hear that Dunmore's inhumanity had even extended to the farm animals, especially horses.

Betsy loved the wild ponies that roamed the Outer Banks. Most of all she loved the beautiful black mare that she had trained from a foal: Black Bess.

The neighbor continued with his tale, "Col. Robert Howe is on his way to Great Bridge. But, it will take a great many more troops than Howe has available to defeat Dunmore. I heard, too, that Col. Isaac Gregory of Camden is hurrying to catch up with the patriots to carry them supplies. Shoot, I doubt with Gregory's small militia they have a chance against Dunmore."

Betsy's father said, "I hear General William Skinner in Perquimans County commands a hundred soldiers. If someone could take Skinner the news, maybe he could get to Great Bridge in time to help Howe and Gregory."

"The way the wind is breezing up to the east, we can't get there fast enough. Come morning we can try it, but by then it will probably be too late," Mr. Jarvis shook his head solemnly.

Betsy tossed and turned in her bed. All she

could think of was Lord Dunmore reaching the Carolinas and slaughtering the Banker ponies. She'd heard her father say, "That renegade will slaughter all our livestock, too. He won't leave a single Banker pony alive. Dunmore is making sure we have no way to pull our wagons to market. Most of all, he is eliminating our Calvary mounts."

When Betsy finally dozed off she was awakened by nightmares of the cruel Lord Dunmore charging over the sand dunes of Currituck after her beloved Black Bess.

Betsy sat straight up in her bed. It was then she made up her mind. She would take Black Bess and go to General Skinner herself. She knew her pony was the fastest on the islands and in the best condition for the long ride. Galloping in the deep sand racing after seagulls had given the pony strength and stamina. If anyone could reach Perquimans by morning, it was her Black Bess. So, Miss Dowdy scribbled a hasty note to her mother explaining her mission. She put it on her pillow.

Betsy crept downstairs, holding her breath

when the old steps creaked under her feet. She sighed with relief when she reached the bottom, then tiptoed out the front door. Quickly and noiselessly she got her pony. Betsy didn't have a saddle. A rustic bridle made of fishnet cord was all the tack she needed. Without a thought of the cold December air, she vaulted onto the pony's back and took off for General Skinner's camp.

Enduring the wet and frigid conditions, Betsy rode over fifty miles, swimming the cold Currituck Sound and riding through the Great Dismal Swamp. She tried not to think of the wild creatures that lived in the swamp as Bess galloped down the narrow foot trail. Betsy rode on through Camden, and then Elizabeth City. Finally they reached the outskirts of Hertford where General William Skinner and his army of one hundred men were encamped.

Cold and exhausted, Betsy told Skinner about Lord Dunmore's plans. The General called his men to arms and they marched north to Great Bridge. They were just in time. On December 11, 1775 Dunmore's army was defeated in a thirty-minute battle, halting his infiltration of North Carolina's coast.

Had it not been for a teenaged girl and her Banker pony, who knows how differently things could have turned out in the American Revolution?

Chapter Three
Saving Corolla's Wild Horses

Headed up by long time horseman, Jerome Barr, a group of mounted men congregated in the small town of Corolla, North Carolina. Looking like they were about to move cattle down the Chisholm Trail, these cowboys had an entirely different mission. They came to round up a herd of wild horses. The horses lived in the yards, streets and marshes surrounding the town situated between Currituck Sound and the Atlantic Ocean.

Until the 1980s Corolla was a small fishing village with only about fifteen homes. There was no road, just a sandy path, and until the 1960's there was no electricity. In 1987 a paved section of Highway 12 was built through Corolla and opened for public use. Within a year of the highway's opening seven wild horses were hit and killed by speeding vehicles; others were injured. The residents saw this as a tragedy and a threat to their heritage.

Fifteen homes grew to fifteen hundred. In addition, shopping centers, condos and other

14

businesses were built. Progress had come to Currituck Banks. Green grass planted alongside the highway, on the golf courses, and in yards attracted the horses. They were often seen grazing in these areas. Tourists began leaving out treats to get the horses to come close enough for photographs. The visitors did not understand that the horses were wild and that they could present a danger.

No one can predict when a horse might feel threatened. In defense, horses bite and kick. While the townspeople were heart broken over the horses that had been killed in traffic, they also worried that eventually a person would be hurt, and consequently a move to destroy the horses might result.

Their concern led to the formation of the Corolla Wild Horse Fund. They organized to raise money that would be used to protect the herd. They put up signs warning motorists of the free roaming horses. The group published a newsletter to help educate tourists about the origin and history of the horses.

After much hard work, and still no public

funding, CWHF members were frustrated when more horses were struck and killed by vehicles. The group knew the only way to protect the horses was to keep them out of the road. They could herd them north to an uninhabited part of the island, but how could they keep them there?

A fence was the answer. It would have to stretch all the way across the island, out into the Currituck Sound on the west side and into the ocean on the east side. It would be expensive. And if that wasn't a big enough problem, they found the idea did not set well with fishermen who wanted to drive their SUVs up the beach to fish. The fence would block their way. Somehow the fence would have to keep horses in, but let the sportsmen through—after all, the beach was public domain.

Someone thought of a cattle guard, the type of bridge ranchers use across canals and creeks. The bridge is made of a metal grid that the cattle are reluctant to walk over, but a vehicle can cross easily. The cattle guard had to be modified so the horses wouldn't get a hoof caught in it. That would be expensive, too. Through t-shirt sales, adopt-a-wild-horse programs and a variety of fund-raisers the money came together and the fence was built. The fishermen accepted the compromise, detouring off the beach and over the cattle guard, then back onto the beach.

Roundup day finally arrived. Under the leadership of Mr. Barr, professional horsemen from surrounding areas volunteered their time to help. They trailered their horses to Corolla, and aided by local people who were on foot, they rounded up the wild horses and herded them through the gate onto the 17,000-acre refuge of public, private, county, state, and federal land.

It became unusual to see horses in the town of Corolla. The herd lived on land that could only be reached on foot or four-wheel drive vehicles. Nine horses, led by a stallion named Little Red Man, lived on a 400-acre island called Dew's Island just off the mainland. The residents of Corolla missed having their wild horses for neighbors but were happy to have them out of harm's way.

But, that was not the end of the story. It wasn't long before the residents of Corolla learned how smart their equine neighbors really were. Herds are broken into small bands that are led by dominant mares. Some of these lead mares were too smart for their own good. They walked across the cattle guard, completely unafraid of the metal and the hollow noise their hooves made when they stepped onto it. The horses were taken back to the refuge and black and yellow stripes were painted on the bridge in hope of scaring the horses from crossing.

Later some of the horses figured out all they had to do was wait for the tide to go out and wade around the end of the fence on the sound-side. They were moved back onto the preserve, but once they learned the way to town there was no way to prevent them from coming back. Once again the headlines told the sad story of wild horses killed or injured in the nighttime traffic. The CWHF members decided to adopt these smart leaders out to private owners. They now live on farms on the mainland.

The next problem CWHF had was keeping

the horses in North Carolina. Since their preserve borders the NC/VA state line the horses unaware they were supposed to stay in North Carolina, would graze their way into the neighboring state. Again, they were found in conflict with town traffic. So, another fence was built on the north end of their refuge at False Cape State Park in the winter of 2003. Volunteers from both states helped construct the fence.

It's a ten-mile hike from the paved road up the beach to the area where the wild horses are living. But you can also go by the ocean shore if you have a four-wheel drive vehicle. Guides charge a fee to take tourists on ATV, four-wheel drive or even by kayak to visit the Corolla wild horses. Be aware that law prohibits people from getting closer than fifty feet from a wild horse. It is unlawful to approach, feed, pet or try to ride the wild horses. Enjoy them from a distance and use your zoom lens for photographs.

Chapter Four
Wreckers and Wild Ponies

Walter Latham watched the flotsam bobbing in the surf. He smiled and then waved to his crew. Three ragtag men came running across the dunes. Each led a pony with a makeshift packsaddle on its back.

"Come on, hurry on, men!" Latham called, "The tide will be coming in soon."

The four men waded out into the ocean and began grabbing hold of crates and barrels of goods and floated them to shore, dragged them up on the beach, and then went back for more.

In the colonial days, the wreckers, as they were called, made a living salvaging debris that washed in from wrecked ships on the shoals along the barrier islands of North Carolina. That bit of geography earned the coast its nickname, Graveyard of the Atlantic, honestly. Men like Walter made a good living gathering the cargo and taking it inland to sell to the merchants of Elizabeth City and Edenton. The merchants never asked the wreckers about their sources for things like sugar, rum, fine

21

silks, and oriental spices. They were only too happy to purchase them at the wrecker's bargain prices.

Standing by, waiting patiently, were three Banker Ponies. They were so called because these hardly little horses were native to the Outer Banks of North Carolina. The men and women who lived by the sea tamed these "wild" horses and used them to pull in fishing nets, transport people and goods across land, and for the sport of horse racing. The ponies played an important role in the hard life of the islanders.

"Okay, Henry and Josiah, let's pack the ponies and be off to the sound shore to load the boats," Walter directed his men.

"Aye, Captain," Josiah answered with a grin. He strapped the contents of one of the crates to the packsaddle while a younger man named Abel held the pony's bridle. Henry worked the other side of the pony until they had the pack balanced. With the three ponies packed to their limits, the men carried what they could on their own backs. They would trek across the sand dunes from ocean side to sound side with sacks of sugar, crates of rum, and bolts of fabric. But, the one thing that excited the men most on this venture was a bunch of ripe bananas.

"What in the world are these?" asked Josiah when they floated up onto the beach.

Abel ran over to look. "Most curious things I ever saw," he said.

Latham's laugher boomed across the beach and a flock of seagulls flew up from their own salvaging at the noise.

"They are bananas! Sweet as honey, they are. Here, try one," he said. Latham peeled one of the fruits and passed it to Josiah, then peeled two more for the others.

"I never tasted anything so delicious. I will take some home to Anna. Where do they come from?" Henry asked Walter.

"The south seas, Florida, the Caribbean. I've heard it said you can live a healthy life on nothing but these bananas. Fruit of the Gods they say."

The men divided the fruit between them to take home to their families.

"A shame about the ship's crew," said Henry, "Apparently none survived this one. T'was a terrible storm last night. Not so lucky as I was ten years ago. Only by God's grace did I not drown when the Isabelle crashed off Piney Island. And only by the grace of God was I found by you, Cap'n Latham. Had those land pirates who lured us into the shoals with their old nag and that lantern tied about her neck found me, they would have slit me throat for sure."

"That they would have. They are an evil bunch. Gives us honest wreckers a bad name, they do. I blame the merchants, too. They know how that bunch of scallywags get their goods, but turn the eye and buy from them anyway," Walter Latham spat on the ground, and shook his head in disgust.

"Well, they won't be profiting from this wreck, sir," said Abel, "and they won't be eating this good fruit called bananas." The young man grinned and turned up the oyster shell path to his house, leading his pony laden with the salvage from the shipwreck. He could hardly wait to share the booty with his wife, Eleanor.

Leading their Banker Ponies, the men headed home, sad at the fate of the ship's crew who lost their lives at sea, but thankful for the bounty that washed ashore. They would make enough money, along with what they made fishing, to care for their families.

Chapter Five
The Devil's Hoof Prints

A popular folk tale of North Carolinians involves a horse of Banker Pony descent. In colonial North Carolina Banker Ponies were crossed with the English Thoroughbred to produce a horse that could sprint a quarter mile race faster than any other horse. Today they are called American Quarter Horses.

The story took place near Bath, North Carolina, the state's oldest town, which is situated on the mainland in Beaufort County just north of the Pamlico River.

A man named Jesse Elliot loved to race his stallion, Thunder, on the local quarter-mile track. He was a bit of a reckless sort whose drinking and betting, as well as racing, caused his wife a great deal of grief. She warned him that these vices were sinful and she prayed for him whenever services were held at St. Thomas Episcopal Church, which still stands today.

One Sunday, as Elliot prepared to saddle his horse and meet his friends at the races, his wife felt a sense of foreboding. She clung to his shirtsleeve and begged him not to go. Mr. Elliot shook her off, and mounted his horse. He galloped away, leaving his wife's cries in the wind.

When he arrived at the stretch of road that served as the racetrack he noticed a stranger there. The man was dressed in black and rode a tall, black horse. He had a somber look about him, which irritated Jesse Elliot. He'd come to have fun: to laugh, tell tall tales, drink and win the race.

"Did you come to race, or just to watch my horse beat all these other horses?" Elliot questioned the man.

The stranger didn't say a word, but walked his horse up to the starting line. For lack of a straight stretch, the road curved around a huge oak tree just a few yards from the finish line The finish line was marked by a rope was stretch across the road, and held on either side by a couple of teenaged boys. The first to break the rope barrier was the winner of the race.

Men, and even a few women, lined both sides

of the quarter-mile stretch, ready to cheer for the horse they hoped would be the winner. Elliot accepted the stranger's unspoken challenge and rode up beside him. Thunder was ready to go, and Elliot had to hold back on the reins. The stranger's horse stood still, as if he had no idea of running down the road to win a race. Elliot grinned. He thought he had this race in the bag.

"Get ready, get set, go!" a man shouted and fired a pistol.

The stranger's horse immediately lunged forward and ahead of Elliot and Thunder. Elliot slapped at his mount's rump with his hat to urge Thunder to run faster. Thunder stretched his legs and gathered them back under, pushing himself forward in powerful strides. But his efforts were not enough; the black horse was keeping his lead.

The people on the sidelines were screaming and waving their hats in the air. Bets were being made back and forth. They were not used to seeing a horse outrun Thunder.

The finish line was getting closer, and the

black horse was still ahead by a length. Elliot cursed and shouted in Thunder's ear, "Take me in a winner, or take me to hell!" He hit the stallion with an angry blow on the shoulder just as they were turning the curve around the oak tree. At that moment Thunder reared, and twisted in mid air. When the stallion came back down his front hooves dug into the packed sand of the road. Elliot's body was propelled forward and his head crashed into the oak tree. He died instantly of a broken neck. At that very moment the stranger's horse crossed the finish line.

The crowd was stunned by what happened. Silence hung in the air like a black cloud. Then they rushed to the scene to see if they could help, but there was nothing they could do. Thunder stood by his master's body and snorted. He tossed his head and turned to look back at the winning horse. But when the crowd looked for the stranger, he nor his horse were anywhere to be seen.

The witnesses declared Elliot had raced with the devil himself and had lost not only the race, but his soul as well.

According to local folks you can still see those hoof prints made by Thunder. Many have tried to bury them or dig them up, but when they return to look, the hoof prints are back. The area was even used for a pigpen, but as soon as the pigs were moved the prints reappeared.

When I was a young child my grandmother from upstate New York came to visit. She loved stories about ghosts and strange phenomenon. When my mother told her the story of the devil's hoof prints she wanted to go to Bath and see them for her self. So, the next day we traveled to the small historic town. We asked directions and found the legendary spot at the base of an ancient oak tree. I don't remember much about what we saw, but my grandmother declared to everyone who would listen that she had indeed seen the devil's hoof prints.

Chapter Six
Gilbert and the Wreck of the Priscilla
(A story based on a historical shipwreck rescue)

The small, brown horse took another bite of sea oats. His teeth made a screnching sound as he pulled at the tough grass. He gazed at the surf pounding the shore while he munched and swallowed.

Gilbert was a Banker Pony. He belonged to Mr. Rasmus Midgett, a surfman serving in the United States Lifesaving Service on the coast of North Carolina. A surfman's job was to patrol the beaches looking for shipwrecks, and then rescue the crewmen and passengers.

On August 16, 1897 the sea was calm and the sky was a deep blue with a few puffy white clouds. But, by the wee hours of the next day one of the worst hurricanes in history crashed into the Carolina coast.

It was three in the morning when Mr. Midgett saddled Gilbert and prepared to ride his shift. The wind had already begun to blow, and by the time they arrived at the Gull Shoal Station it was raining. Donned in a slicker and hat, he drank a hot cup of

31

coffee before starting his seven-mile patrol.

The surfmen of the Outer Banks were the only ones in the country allowed to ride horseback while patrolling the beaches. The rules were that they only walk the horses, except in an emergency. Gilbert had been walking over an hour with waves crashing around his feet and washing the sand out from under them. Once he stumbled, then regained his balance and kept on going. By now the wind was howling and mixing the rain with sand that peppered the faces of Gilbert and his human partner. Gilbert lowered his head and flattened his ears while Mr. Midgett pulled his collar tighter around his neck and his hat down over his forehead. They leaned into the wind and continued down the beach.

The storm raged with a vengeance. The waves got higher and the wind blew foam through the air. A huge wave hit Gilbert broadside and almost toppled him over. Gilbert was struggling to walk. When the next wave crashed against the beach and washed back out to sea something bumped hard against Gilbert's legs.

"What was that?" Mr. Midgett reined Gilbert to a stop and peered into the surf.

"A barrel." Midgett looked into the surf swirling around Gilbert's feet and saw the object bobbing in the waves. There were more being tossed onto the beach; some were broken open and the contents spilled out.

Gilbert stopped again; he heard a noise. It wasn't the wind or the surf. His ears switched from side to side.

"I hear it, too, Gil," Mr. Midgett said as he peered from under his hat, holding tight so it didn't blow away. Then he pulled it back down over his head and urged Gilbert to walk on.

The litter of cargo was all along the beach, more bobbed in the churning waters.

"Help!" the sound came across the ocean from the darkness. Gilbert turned his head in the direction of the sound. Lightning split the darkness in two and Gilbert could see the broken hull of a ship. The waves beat against the boat, and pounded it further onto the shoals.

"Shipwreck!" Mr. Midgett drew up on Gilbert's reins. He stood in the stirrups and peered into the blackness, trying to see how many were on the deck. He called out in a deep voice, "How many?"

Someone shouted back, "Ten living, four drowned!"

"All right, Gilbert, we have to handle this. There's not time to go for help; that will take two hours. By then, all will have perished. Wait here, Gil." Mr. Midgett dismounted and walked into the water. He waited until the waves washed back, and then ran across the wet sand toward the sinking ship.

Gilbert waited right where Mr. Midgett left him. He stood with his rear legs pulled underneath him; held his head low and flattened his ears to shut out the pelting rain. Pine branches and tuffs of seaweed sailed around him, tossed by the howling wind. The swirling sand stung his legs like a swarm of bees. Shivering with cold and fear, Gilbert wanted to run and hide, but he waited.

One by one Mr. Midgett followed the waves

out to sea and had the sailors jump off the ship, and then he swam them back to shore. The last three men were injured. They couldn't jump. They dropped a line to Mr. Midgett, he climbed aboard the ship and carried the three remaining men back down the line and to safety.

He wrapped the injured Captain Springsteen in his coat and made sure the rescued victims were safe at the base of a sand dune. The four missing people were the captain's wife, first mate and his two sons. They'd washed overboard in the storm.

Finally, Mr. Midgett turned to Gilbert.

"Good boy," he said and rubbed the horse's neck. Then he swung into the saddle. Their work was not done.

"All right, fella, let's hurry back to the station. These people need warm shelter and medical attention."

He squeezed his legs and Gilbert leaped into a gallop. The little horse ran across the wet sand, gathering his legs under himself, then stretching out in long ground covering strides. Time was in short supply. All of the survivors, especially the three injured men, were suffering from the cold and rain. Gilbert didn't falter or slow his pace until he and Mr. Midgett saw a yellow light appear through the driving rain.

The surfman leaned forward and whispered in the horse's ear, "We're almost there, Gil. Almost there." When they reached the oyster shell path that led to the station he pulled on the reins and brought Gilbert down to a trot, then to a stop. Mr. Midgett dismounted and bounded up the four steps to the front door. He shook the wet off and wiped his feet, then opened the screened door. The wind grabbed the door and slammed it against the gray-shingled wall. Midgett pulled it shut behind him as he entered the hallway.

Again, Gilbert stood and waited for his master. Moments later Mr. Midgett ran outside with two other men. He led Gilbert to the stable and put him in a stall, while the other men hitched two horses to carts.

Gilbert had munched his hay and was dozing

when he heard the carts pull back into the yard with the injured men. The rest of the victims walked along the side of the carts. They were taken inside the station house where Mr. Midgett and the other crewmen made them warm and comfortable. Soon all was quiet as the exhausted sailors went to sleep. Mr. Midgett's shift was over, and so was the storm. He was suddenly aware of his aching muscles.

"Well, boy. It was a long night, let's go home and get some rest," he said.

The sun was shinning, and the sea was slick and calm, the only sign of the raging storm was the debris scattered along the beach. A lone seagull sailed through the clear, blue sky and dived into the sea. It came back up with a small, silver fish. Gilbert was glad to be going home, leaving a trail of hoof prints in the sand to be washed away by the waves.

(A copy of the report filed on the rescue of the Priscilla can be found at the Outer Banks History Center in Manteo, NC at Festival Park)

Chapter Seven
How Nags Head Got its Name

The light swayed rhythmically, its yellow glow appearing and disappearing with the rise and fall of the ocean's waves, or so it seemed. The ship's watchman called out, pointing toward the light, "Ship to the starboard!"

The captain sighed with relief. The sight of another vessel meant they were in safe waters. The storm had blown them off course, and he'd worried they were too close to shore. All who sailed to the New World knew the reputation of these waters near the Carolina coast—the Graveyard of the Atlantic. The hidden sand bars and frequent storms made navigation a perilous and death-defying job.

The captain's relief was nullified when the ship shuddered and groaned to a stop. It had run aground. The captain cursed. He instantly knew the truth about the light, but it was too late. The nag's head had doomed him and his crew. The storm beat the ship against the shoal and it soon shattered into thousands of matchstick pieces. Some of the crew may have made it to shore, but it was more likely that they all perished in the sea. The ship's valuable cargo floated and bobbed in the churning waves. Eventually the pounding waves washed most of it to the beach.

The "nag's head" was an evil trick performed by land pirates who found the barrier islands off the coast of North Carolina a perfect refuge. A lantern tied around the neck of one of the horses that lived on the islands lured passing ships in close to the shallows. A stormy night presented the best time for the evil deed. Then they simply led the horse up and down the ridges of sand dunes. The unsuspecting seaman would mistake the lantern's light for a ship's light and believe they were in deep water, safe from running aground. By the time the ship's captain realized his mistake the ship was stuck in the sand and it was all over. If it was not a stormy night the pirates came on board and made their raid, stealing the precious cargo and murdering the crew. But the storm made things even easier for the pirates. They just waited till morning to salvage what cargo washed ashore.

The ponies were likely used to pull wagons or carry packs of the wares collected by the thieves to the sound side of the island. Then the pirates loaded the cargo in their boats they kept hidden in the sounds and creeks behind the islands. They sold the stolen goods to colonial merchants on the mainland, who asked no questions.

The merchants could buy at much lower cost from the pirates than from legitimate suppliers and make a larger profit for themselves. Being a land pirate was less risky than working on the high seas. Some pirates got so rich that they bought plantations on the mainland and lived as "respectable" citizens.

Meanwhile, word spread back to Europe about the tricky land pirates. As sailors were about to embark on a voyage they were warned, "Beware of the nag's head." Soon that area of the Outer Banks became known as Nags Head. The name stuck, and the area is now one of the world's most popular resort areas. The wild ponies used by the pirates for their dastardly deeds at Nags Head no longer roam the area, but figurines symbolizing the poor nag can be purchased in almost every gift shop in town.

Chapter Eight
Captain Howard's Mounted Boy Scout Troop
(Based on an interview with Mr. Rudy Austin)

Rudy raised his cap to the crowd and gave Diablo a secret cue. The pony reared up and pawed the air. Rudy grinned and the people applauded.

Performing at the Pirate Jamboree in Buxton, North Carolina was just one of the activities that Rudy and other members of Captain Marvin Howard's Mounted Boy Scout Troop enjoyed in the 1950s. They also went on camping trips, hunting, and as a community service project they rode into the marshes on horseback to spray for mosquitoes. Captain Marvin Howard's Mounted Boy Scout Troop was the first mounted troop in the United States.

Before a boy could join this special Boy Scout troop, he had to catch a wild horse and train it. The horses were from a herd that ran free among the sand dunes of Ocracoke Island on the coast of North Carolina.

Descended from horses left on the islands by Spanish explorers, the ponies adapted well to the area. By the twentieth century several hundred lived on the remote island of Ocracoke.

Captain Marvin Howard organized the troop in 1956 after he retired from a career as a sailor. It was something he'd dreamed of doing for a long time. He believed the boys and horses would make a perfect match.

To catch their mounts most boys used food to win the horses' confidence. Next came teaching them to lead, then accepting a bridle and bit.

When a horse was used to the weight of a saddle on his back the last step was to ride. Sometimes, if a horse was especially spunky, the Boy Scout used an old Indian method, which was to lead the horse out into the water, then the rider floated onto the horse's back. That way if he fell off he'd have a soft landing.

***

A few years after the troop was formed, North Carolina passed a law saying all free-roaming livestock, including horses, had to be removed from the island. The legislators were afraid the livestock would eat all of the grass on the sand dunes and cause the island to wash away. The grass and sea oats prevented beach erosion.

Captain Marvin and other local citizens convinced the lawmakers to make an exception for the boys' horses.

Under the new law, the boys could no longer let their horses run free to graze. They had to keep them corralled. This made the horses more expensive to keep since they had to be fed grain and hay. Fewer boys were able to afford the horses and the troop eventually disbanded, in spite of Captain Marvin's efforts to keep the horses from being moved off the island.

"It was a fantastic boyhood," says Mr. Rudy Austin, "We knew it then, but appreciate it even more looking back."

Ocracoke Island is part of the Cape Hatteras National Seashore. A herd of about twenty wild ponies are now kept inside a 160-acre fenced pasture to keep them safe from traffic and to prevent them from grazing on the sand dunes. They are descended from a group of horses purchased by Mr. Sam Jones at the last roundup in the late 1950s. Mr. Jones then donated them to the park service so future generations could enjoy seeing the wild horses of Ocracoke, an important part of the island's heritage.

The pasture is located 6.2 miles south of the Hatteras – Ocracoke ferry landing on highway 12. Visitors can see the "Banker Ponies," as they were called in the days of Captain Marvin, from an observation tower next to the pen.

Chapter Nine
Betsy Dowdy Looks for Pirate Treasure
(A fictional story based on the character of Besty Dowdy)

Betsy Dowdy lived on an island on the coast of North Carolina in the 1700s. She had a Banker Pony named Black Bess. Betsy and Bess are legendary for their daring ride to warn, "The British are coming!" on December 6, 1775. My book, *An Independent Spirit,* is based on the legend of Betsy Dowdy and Black Bess.

We can only imagine how the freedom of living on North Carolina's Outer Banks gave Betsy the opportunity for many other adventures. Many children living near the coast have dug for pirate's treasure. I remember my own determination to find Black Beard's gold right in my backyard. I gave up after hours of digging. Like Betsy, I learned the treasure of living in Eastern North Carolina had nothing to do with gold.

"Look, Bess. I brought you a treat. Mother made corn fritters this morning." Betsy held her hand out to the black pony, careful to not let Bess get a finger along with the treat.

Bess nudged Betsy's hand to see if there was a second piece.

"No, that's all. Mother said I shouldn't waste her good cooking on a horse, so I just took one piece. Come on girl, we are going on a treasure hunt." Betsy slipped the bridle onto Bess and hopped onto her back. She didn't have a saddle, but that was fine. Betsy rode like she was part of Bess, always balanced, and she hardly ever fell off. When she did fall off Bess waited for her to get back on and away they'd go like the wind.

Betsy guided her pony toward the sound side of the island along a narrow path between the tall sea oats and live oak trees. She talked to her pony along the way, every once in a while leaning down to pat Bess on the shoulder, or sometimes she'd reach back and scratch her pony on the rump.

"I was listening to Father and Mr. Davenport talking on the front porch last night. They were telling tales about pirates. Mr. Davenport said there is pirate treasure buried all over these islands. He said whoever found it would be richer than the governor himself."

Betsy gave Bess another pat on the neck and said, "We are going to look for treasure, yes we are. I asked him where he thought it might be? He said if he were a pirate he'd bury it far enough from shore that the tide wouldn't wash it out, and he'd look for a landmark to help him find it later. Of course we know the pirates were arrested and they couldn't come back to find their treasure. It must still be buried right here on our island.

"Last night I hardly slept a wink puzzling about where I would bury treasure if I were a pirate. Then I fell asleep and I had a dream. I dreamed I was hiding in the myrtle thicket watching a whole gang of pirates dig a big hole just ten paces from the base of that big, crooked oak tree up the hill from Blackberry Bay. You know? Right where I climb up into the branches and eat my lunch when we go to the bay to fish and swim."

Betsy ducked under a scuppernong vine that grew across the path and then turned Bess to the right when the path divided. They went left along the water's edge, and then up the slope of a sandy hill covered with trees and shrubs. When they got to the top Betsy reined Bess to a stop and dismounted. They were standing next to a big tree. The limbs were twisted and bent low, shaped by the wind for many years. The base of the trunk was thicker than any of the other trees in the forest. One branch dipped close enough to the ground that Betsy could sit on it and her toes still touched the sand.

But Betsy didn't have time for sitting on this day. She had digging to do. She took the bridle off Bess to let her pony graze. Then Betsy stood close to the tree trunk and began to take giant steps toward the sound. One, two, three she counted and stopped when she got to ten.

Betsy took a big cooking spoon out of her pocket and got down on her knees and began digging. Bess looked at her friend a moment. Was she digging for water? Bess sometimes dug a hole with her hooves and waited for fresh water to seep into the hole to drink. But they were too far up the hill to dig for water. The pony resumed eating grass and Betsy kept digging. She knew it would take a long time to dig deep enough to find treasure with a spoon, even if it was a big cooking spoon.

The sun rose higher in the sky. It was getting hot even in the shade of the big tree. Betsy wished she had brought some water to drink and a lunch. She'd been so excited about finding buried treasure she'd forgotten. Well, as least Black Bess was eating lunch. She'd been grazing all morning. Betsy kept on digging. But all she was finding was sand and more sand.

Betsy was getting tired. She thought Bess might be thirsty. "Let's take a break, Bess. We'll ride down to the sound and you can get a drink. Maybe I'll find some grapes. I am hungry." She put the bridle back on her pony and hopped onto her back.

The two friends followed the path back down the hill and along the sound. The sound water was brackish, but not as salty as the ocean on the other side of the island. Bess stopped a few feet from the shore and pawed the sand with one of her front feet.

Soon the hole she made filled with water and Bess took a drink. Betsy picked some grapes to eat. Soon she was ready to dig some more. She rode Bess back to the top of the hill. When she looked at the hole she'd dug that morning it didn't look very deep.

"At this pace we'll never find any treasure, Bess." Black Bess snickered and kept munching grass. Betsy wasn't sure, but she thought her pony was laughing at her. "You are right. Grandpa was probably just making up tales. There's no buried treasure here. Let's go home."

Betsy hopped onto the pony's back once again and turned her around. They started back home. The sky was dotted with white, cottony clouds. When they came out of the woods Betsy rode Bess along the ocean shore. Green waves rolled in and crashed onto the sand sending sprays of sea foam through the air. It felt cool on Betsy's face. Some seagulls swooped down to the wet sand to quickly gobble up the tiny fish and crabs that had washed in with the waves. The gulls sounded like they were laughing. Betsy urged her pony into a gallop down the beach. Both her long hair and Bess's mane and tail were flying in the wind.

When she saw a school of dolphins playing in the surf she reined Bess to a stop. She sat and watched. The sea mammals did cartwheels in the water just beyond the breakers and Betsy laughed. She looked down the long span of golden sand. The light from the sun and the moisture from the surf made the sand sparkle and twinkle like a million little diamonds.

"Bess, who needs pirate treasure? We have all the beauty of gold and jewels right here before us. What could money from treasure buy us that would be better than going to sleep to the music of the ocean's song and waking up to the glorious sunrises that turn our world into a wonderland of crimson and gold. What could replace my rides with you across the sand and in the forests of live oak and myrtle trees, doing chores with Mother and sitting on the front porch listening to Father tell us tall tales? We live in the best place of all the colonies, don't we Bess?" Betsy leaned down and gave her pony a hug

53

around the neck. Bess turned her head back and looked at Betsy, then nodded as if in agreement.

"Bess, we have plenty of treasure right here."

Chapter Ten
Going to the County Fair
(A fictional story based on a newspaper report of North Carolina's first "oyster, fish and game fair.")

"Betsy, you're going to be the prettiest Banker Pony at the fair," Margaret said as she brushed her pony's black mane vigorously. "If you win the show you'll get a big blue ribbon and your name in the Weekly." The pony snorted and shook her head as if in anticipation.

It was the fall of 1887. Margaret lived in a small community called Cedar Island on the coast of North Carolina. Her father had bought Betsy as a yearling at the July 4th pony auction four years earlier. Every July 4th there was a pony penning. All the horses were rounded up and corralled; some were auctioned to the highest bidders. Betsy was trained to pull a cart, plow the garden, and help pull in the fishing nets.

What Margaret loved to do most of all was take long rides on the beach with Betsy. Strolling through woods and grasses and over the dunes to the shore she'd have long talks with her pony, who listened and kept all of her secrets. When the tide was out, the wet sand was packed and made good footing. Then Margaret would lean forward and whisper to her pony, "Let's go girl!" And Betsy would take off in a full gallop, scattering the seagulls along their way. Then she'd rein her pony down to a trot, and trotting they did go. Margaret would urge Betsy to go fast as she could without breaking back into a gallop. She always walked Betsy back home to cool her pony down by the time they got there.

Sometimes the waves were big and came crashing to shore spraying the rider and horse with sea spray. Margaret loved the feeling of the wind in her hair, the smell of the sea, and the laughing of the gulls. She knew she lived in the best place on earth.

Some of the wild horses of Cedar Island were owned by people on the islands and had their brands on their hips. Some horses not yet claimed were auctioned off. The horses were dipped in insecticide to get rid of ticks and turned back out into the marshes after the pennings. The horses earned the name "marsh tackies" because they lived in the marshes eating the tough grasses that grew there.

"You and Daddy might win the trotter race. You are pretty fast. I know you are the prettiest horse on the island, or the whole world for that matter. I think you will win the contest for the most beautiful and stylish." Margaret brushed the tangles out of Betsy's long, shiny mane. Then she began braiding it in long, thin braids. Margaret worked all afternoon until the sun started to set on the sound side of the island.

"There," she gave her pony a pat, "tomorrow, when I take down your braids and brush them out you will have beautiful, wavy hair. I'll tie in some red ribbons after the race. I just know you will win the beauty contest.

Margaret led Betsy to the little stable behind the house and put her in the stall next to Minnie, their milk cow. She filled their mangers with hay and gave Betsy a measure of oats. She remembered how she'd had to teach the pony to eat hay and oats when they first got her home. Betsy was used to the wild grasses in the marshes and had never had hay or grain before coming to live with Margaret's family.

Daddy would drive Betsy in the race. Margaret planned to leave Betsy's braids in until afterwards. She would be prepared with a towel to rub the pony down and clean off the sweat, and then she'd brush out her mane and tie in the red ribbons. Butterflies danced in her tummy thinking about going to the fair. It was North Carolina's first Oyster, Fish and Game Fair.

Margaret's mama was entering produce from their garden in a competition– turnips, corn, and squash. She was also entering her blueberry pie in the baking contest. Mama packed the picnic basket with fried chicken, potato salad, and biscuits with strawberry jam. She was worried her family would get hungry during the day, even though that evening there would be a big fish fry and oyster roast.

When they arrived it was the most exciting thing Margaret had ever experienced. She'd never seen so many people in one place in her whole life. Families from all over the island and from the mainland gathered in an open field, which now was lined with canopies that shaded tables for the fruits, vegetables, jams, jellies, pies, and cakes that were entered in the various competitions. Adjoining the field was an oval track for the races. A booth next to the track for registering the horses had a big sign tacked on the front announcing two divisions: one for pacers and the other for trotters. Margaret went with her daddy to register Betsy in the trotting division. She gave the pony another quick brush over, patted her and whispered, "Good luck," in Betsy's ear. Betsy nodded her head just like she understood exactly what was expected of her.

"The races start in an hour," Mr. Davis said. "You have time to go look around after we register Betsy in the race and the contest."

"Papa, I will stay to help harness Betsy and keep her company," Margaret said. "I'll have time after we are finished with the horse competitions to see the rest of the fair."

"All right, she can graze a little while you keep an eye on her." Margaret's Daddy went to the hand pump and filled a bucket with water and carried it back to where Margaret and Betsy waited.

Time passed quickly. Soon the race was called. First the pacers lined up at the starting line. A man called out, "Get ready, get set, GO!" and shot a pistol into the air. The horses took off. A chestnut gelding named Sam won the pacing race.

Daddy took Betsy to the lineup for the trotting race. Margaret and her mother, who had joined them when she heard the race called, took a spot on the rail right next to the finish line. Margaret's heart was beating so hard she could hear it.

There were ten horses in the line-up. When the pistol shot rang through the air; Margaret and her mother leaned over the rail to get a better look. Betsy and another mare named Maude T shot out ahead of the rest. A third horse that Margaret didn't know was close behind them. Behind it was a black gelding with four white socks named Piper. He belonged to a neighbor down the road from Margaret's family. Betsy and Maude T were neck and neck halfway down the track. Margaret and her mother were both jumping up and down screaming, "Go Betsy, go!"

Betsy's ears perked forward and her legs stretched out in long two-beat trotting strides. Never breaking her gait, she inched ahead of Maude-T. "That a girl, Betsy!" Margaret yelled. Mrs. Davis clapped her hands and shouted, "Come on, come on!" The horses were a quarter of the way to the finish line. Piper had moved up to third. The other horse had tired and fallen behind to the fifth spot. Maude-T caught up to Betsy again. They were nose and nose. Margaret and her mother jumped up and down, shouting and waving their arms.

"You can do it, Betsy!" But Maude-T was inching ahead of Betsy. The finish line was just a few yards away. "Trot on!" Mrs. Davis yelled.

Betsy gained her position next to Maude-T, and then Maude-T seemed to get a burst of power just before the finish. She won the race. Betsy was second and Piper came in a close third. The race was over.

Margaret and her mother ran down to the far end of the track to meet her father and Betsy. A red ribbon was tied to Betsy's bridle. Margaret gave her pony a hug. "You were wonderful!" she said.

"Papa you were, too. You and Betsy made a fine team." Then Margaret turned to the winner and said, "Maude-T you ran a great race! But, watch out next year. Betsy and I will be training hard until then." She laughed and shook the hand of Maude-T's owner. "Fantastic race," she said.

"Well, we better get Betsy prettied up for the final competition," said Mrs. Davis.

Margaret took the reins and led Betsy back to the holding area. She unharnessed and let her pony drink from the water bucket. She rubbed her down and gave her a good brushing. She unbraided the mane and brushed some more. Then she tied in the red ribbons.

"Well, Papa and Mama, what do you think? Do we have a chance?" Margaret stood back so her parents could get a good look at Betsy.

"Beautiful, and yes, I think Betsy has a very good chance," said her mother.

"Well, she looks mighty fine," said Mr. Davis, "but just remember to be a good sport no matter who wins."

Margaret smiled and took a deep breath. The first class was for the younger horses, three and under. An elegant gray filly won that class. Now it was their turn. The four and over age group was being called. Margaret smoothed Betsy's forelock and started leading her toward the track. The horses were led in a big circle around the judge. Then they lined up side by side in the middle of the track. The judge walked around each horse, making notes on a pad of paper. When He got to Betsy he smiled. He ran his hand down Betsy's back, stood back and looked at her for what seemed to Margaret a very long time. She took another deep breath and exhaled slowly.

Then the judge stood out in front of the line of horses, giving them another last look before he handed his list to the steward.

The steward began calling out names starting with fifth place. Each time a name was called and it wasn't Betsy, Margaret sighed with relief, keeping her fingers crossed behind her back that Betsy would be saved for first place. Now it was time – the next name would be the winner.

"First place goes to . . . ." the steward paused for what seemed like forever, then he said, "Betsy, owned by Margaret Davis!"

Margaret felt tears start to roll down her face. She gave Betsy a big hug around the neck. Then she led her pony forward to receive the blue ribbon. She heard her mother and papa shout out, "Yay! Margaret and Betsy!" Then everyone was clapping.

Margaret led Betsy around the rest of the fair after the crowd finally left the track area. She'd attached the blue ribbon to Betsy's bridle. When they got to the baked goods tent they found Mother's blueberry pie had won the blue ribbon.

Margaret and her parents got in line for the seafood – fried fish, steamed shrimp, oysters, and clams with hush puppies and coleslaw. Margaret thought how lucky they were to live near the sea where this wonderful food was plentiful.

The sun was setting on the sound side, turning the sky gold and rose. Margaret was tired and ready to get home to her bed. She would hang Betsy's ribbons on the wall right over her headboard.

Chapter Eleven
History of the Cedar Island Horses

Cedar Island lies between the Pamlico Sound and Core Banks forty miles northeast of Beaufort, North Carolina. In 1964 over 14,000 acres of Cedar Island was designated a National Wildlife Refuge. The island has a small fishing community and the landing for the Cedar Island to Ocracoke ferry. Historians tell us there were once six hundred horses living in the marshes of Cedar Island. A small herd remains there today.

Evidently, the ponies were a valuable commodity in the nineteenth century. In the December 12, 1884 issue of the *Carteret County Telephone Beaufort Weekly* it was announced that on Cedar Island "We have as fine ponies here as the county affords, which we offer for sale on reasonable terms." Even earlier in the May 17, 1876 issue of the *Beaufort Eagle* an ad from Davis & Bros. offers for sale "40 Bank Ponies." In that same issue there is mention of the pony penning at Jacks on Bell Island the next Saturday, May 20.

Another penning was held in July on Cape Banks. Readers were urged to visit the lighthouse for a birds-eye view of the Atlantic of the ponies they could buy. Boat transportation was provided from Morehead and Beaufort for a "reasonable fee."

In 1887 Carteret County held North Carolina's first "oyster, fish and game fair." Ponies played a key role at this county fair where awards were given in a variety of categories including porpoise products, ear corn, cotton and turnips. Banker Ponies were awarded prizes in several classes. "Maude T." won for fastest trotter and "Sam" was fastest pacer. But it was "Betsy" who was the big winner – she got first place for style and beauty and was named best pony over four-years-old. This may also have been North Carolina's first horse show.

There used to be so many ponies on the island that its one motel had to put up a pony-proof fence to keep the horses from coming onto the grounds and bothering the motel guests. Today, it is rare to see a horse on Cedar Island. The best way to see them is to go into the marshes by kayak. Locals say the horses seem to be able to "walk on water" never getting mired down the way humans do who try to walk out into the marsh.

In January 2003, five horses rounded up from nearby Shackleford were moved to Cedar Island to replenish that herd. By 2010, the herd had grown to thirty-nine.

Chapter Twelve
Go Get Mis Bashi
*(A fictional Story based on the real Basheba Foster
and her Banker Pony, Napoleon)*

The wind whistled around the corner of the pony
shed. Inside Rose Phelps curried her Banker Pony,
Breeze.

"Breeze, the wind is blowing cold tonight. I
hope Papa gets in with the boat before this storm gets
full blown." Breeze munched the hay Rose dropped
in the manger. He flicked his left ear to show he was
listening.

"I'll be right back with a fresh pail of water.
You better stay in tonight; it is going to get rough."

Rose ran through the sea oats and along the
oyster shell path to the back porch. There she
pumped water into the bucket with the hand pump. It
was heavy, but she managed to carry the filled bucket
back to the shed without spilling it.

"Here you go. This will be enough until
morning," she told Breeze as she hung the bucket
onto a hook near the manger.

"I know Mama is worried about Papa getting

in ahead of this storm," Rose confided to her pony. Just as she said the word "storm" lightning flashed and thunder rolled across the dunes. "I think she is worried the baby will come tonight, too. There is a full moon. She says babies like to be born during the full moon. I just hope Papa gets home before that happens."

Rose gave Breeze a pat on his rump. Then she put away the brushes. "Good night, Breeze."

Breeze snorted to answer her, then dropped his head back into the manger full of hay.

"Mama, that chowder sure smells good." Rose hung her coat on the peg next to back door and slipped off her boots.

"Your daddy will need something hot when he gets in. I hope that will be soon. I hate when they are out in rough water. Wash your hands and sit down."

Rose sat down, bowed her head to say a blessing. She sipped a spoonful of the creamy soup. It had a medley of seafood including fish, shrimp and crabmeat with chunks of potato. They ate well all year round from what the sea provided and what they grew in the garden.

"Mm, this is so good, Mama."

"I'm glad you like it." Mama said as she took a pan of cornbread out of the oven. She cut it in squares and put them on a plate. She passed the plate to Rose."

"Thank you, Mama." Rose spread butter on a piece of the hot cornbread.

Rose looked up and saw her mama clench the back of a chair with both hands and frown.

"Mama, are you all right?" Rose asked.

"Yes, yes, I am fine. Just had a little pain. It's nothing. Gone already." Mama resumed washing the cornbread pan, dried it and put it away.

Rose chattered between spoonsful of chowder, mostly talking about Breeze. "We had a nice ride on the beach, but when the wind picked up I was cold so we came back in. I brushed him down real good and gave him some hay and water. I think with the storm it would be better if he stays in tonight."

71

"Oh my goodness, Rose. Those Banker Ponies have been fairing just fine on the beaches during storms for hundreds of years. Breeze's ancestors have weathered many storms worse than this one. You are just making more work for yourself keeping him closed in. You'll have a stall to clean in the morning."

"I don't mind that. I just feel better knowing he's in out of the cold rain and the wind."

Rose noticed her mother grimace again. "Mama are you sure you are all right?"

"Well, yes, but I've had this pain come and go for the last hour or so. I think the baby might be planning to be born tonight." Mama sat down in the chair across from Rose. She smiled.

"I'll be fine, don't look so worried, Rose."

"Really!" Rose was excited now that she knew what was causing her mama's discomfort. Then she felt scared. She had no idea what to do to help bring a baby into the world.

"Mama, what should I do? Tell me." Rose was close to tears.

"Well, I do need for you to do something. Go get Breeze and ride down to Mis Bashi's. Tell her it is time and we need her to come. Go get Mis Bashi!"

Everyone knew Mis Bashi, whose real name was Bathsheba Foster. Mis Bashi was a midwife, a very important person on the island of Hatteras. She had helped deliver babies on the island for decades. She'd help deliver Rose, so Rose could truly say she'd known Mis Bashi from the day she was born.

Mrs. Bathsheba Foster lived alone in a little cottage on the Pamlico Sound, not far from where Rose and her family lived. Not only did she help with birthing babies, she often nursed the sick and injured back to health when there was no doctor on the island.

"All right, Mama." Rose jumped up from her seat, pulled on her boots and grabbed her coat. "I'll be back with Mis Bashi in a jiffy."

Rose was halfway down the path when she saw a light bobbing ahead and heard voices. It was Aunt Twilla and Mrs. Overton carrying a lantern to light their way.

"We are coming to sit with your Mother. It is a full moon and the baby is coming tonight," Aunt Twilla said.

"I'm going for Mis Bashi right now," Rose told the ladies, "she's having some labor pains. I left Breeze in the stall so I'll be quick. Thank you for coming. I know Mama is worried about Papa."

Another streak of lightning ripped through the sky.

"Go, go on girl!" Mrs. Overton said.

The ladies ran toward the house while Rose ran to get her pony.

Rose put the bridle on Breeze. She didn't have a saddle; she didn't need one. She'd always ridden bareback. She led her pony out of the stall and hopped on his back.

In the pouring rain Breeze galloped down the path toward the sound shore. Soon Rose saw a yellow light shining in the window of Mis Bashi's cottage. Before Rose stopped Breeze in the front yard Mis Bashi was standing on the porch.

"It's your mother's time. I expected it would

be tonight. I'll get Napoleon hooked up to the cart and be on my way. Go ahead home, tell your mother I am on my way," the tall, elegant woman said.

"I will, Mis Bashi. Thank you, Ma'am." Rose turned her pony back to go home. Again the pony galloped, ears flattened against the rain.

By the time Rose got home and put her pony back in the stall she heard Napoleon, the midwife's Banker Pony, trotting up the oyster shell path. Mis Bashi got out of the cart and hurried inside the house. Napoleon stood still right where Mis Bashi stopped him. He would wait patiently for her to come back. When Rose followed behind her she saw all of the neighborhood ladies were sitting around the kitchen table. It was tradition on the island for the women of the island to give their support and prayers while a mother was giving birth to her baby. Rose sat down next to Aunt Twilla, who gave her hand a squeeze.

"Don't you worry. Your mama is going to be just fine with Mis Bashi. I remember the night you were born. It was a full moon just like tonight. Your mama didn't have a bit of trouble with your coming into the world. She will do just fine with your new baby sister or brother."

"Thank you, Aunt Twilla. I just wish Papa was here."

"We are all praying for his safe return. Don't worry." Aunt Twilla gave Rose a hug.

Just at that moment Rose heard a baby cry. She looked at her aunt and grinned.

"That's the baby!" she said.

All of the ladies laughed, some had tears rolling down their faces. Tears of joy.

A moment later all was quiet except for the sound of rain pounding on the roof. Then the door to Rose's parents' room opened. Mis Bashi came out holding a little bundle in her arms.

"It's a boy," she said, "and the mother is well."

Rose jumped up from her chair and squealed.

"May I see him?" she asked.

"Of course you may," said Mis Bashi, "Come here and hold him. You are his big sister."

The baby was wrapped in a soft blanket that

Rose had knitted for him. Mis Bashi handed Rose her new baby brother.

"Oh, he is so sweet. I can't wait until he is big enough that I can teach him to ride," Rose said.

Mis Bashi laughed. "Well, I think you have a little while to wait.

Just then the front door swung open. In came Rose's Papa.

"Look, Papa! The baby came. He is a boy!" Rose held up her little brother for her father to see.

Mr. Phelps smiled, then looked at the midwife. "Is she all right? Can I see her?" he asked.

"She is fine. Tired, but just fine. Go see her, and take your son with you."

He took the baby from Rose and stepped into the bedroom.

"Mis Bashi, I will go brush Napoleon down good and give him some hay. He can stay in the shed with Breeze until you are ready to go home," Rose said.

"Thank you, Rose. That is very kind of you."

"Aunt Twilla, we have a pot of chowder on

the stove. Would you give some to Mis Bashi and all the ladies? I know you all missed your supper coming to be with Mama."

"I am going to go take care of the ponies, then I'll come back and wash the dishes, "Rose said. She could hardly keep from just squealing with happiness, but she knew that would wake the baby and her Mama.

Chapter Thirteen
Who was Mrs. Bathsheba Foster?

Mrs. Bathsheba Foster, known lovingly as Mis Bashi by the people on Hatteras Island on the Outer Banks of North Carolina, took care of expecting mothers and their babies and the sick or injured in her community for forty-five years. During this time she cared for her children, her ailing mother, and her brother's children. In addition she managed to run a small farm with cows and pigs and kept a garden. Her Banker Pony, Napoleon, pulled a small cart and that is how she got around the island to make calls on those who needed her. He was descended from the Spanish horses that were brought to America by European explorers and colonists in the 1500s.

Mis Bashi had little formal education and did not know how to read. But she taught herself to be a midwife. In 1923 a woman doctor, Blanche Nettleton Epler, came and stayed on the island for ten years. The two women worked together, combining both the old traditional midwifery and the doctor's modern medical knowledge to care for the people of

Hatteras Island. After Dr. Epler left, Mis Bashi continued serving the community. You can read more about Mis Bashi and Dr. Epler in *A Historian's Coast* by David Cecelski.

Chapter Fourteen
Fourth of July Parade
(A fictional story based on a true event)

Long ribbons of Spanish moss hung from the live oak trees and swayed in the hot South Carolina summer breeze. Toby and Laurie Leigh Jordan were sweating, but they didn't mind. It was July 4th and they were helping the family pack the station wagon with lawn chairs, towels, and a cooler filled with sodas, fried chicken, deviled eggs and Mama's famous potato salad. They were headed to town for the big parade and then a picnic on the beach.

"Look! There are the Marsh Tackies!" Laurie Leigh pointed to some horses in a pasture as they passed by. "Do you think there will be horses in the parade?"

"I'm sure there will be horses," Mama assured her horse-crazy daughter.

"I bet those Marsh Tackies wish they could be in the parade. After all, they are South Carolina's oldest horses," Toby said.

"Yep, they've been here longer than any other horses. They were the first horses to come to

America." Laurie Leigh had written a report for her social studies class about Marsh Tackies and knew all about them. She knew they descended from horses brought to the New World by Spanish Explorers in the 16th century.

"Well, we can be thankful a few people are breeding them and keeping them off the beaches or there wouldn't be any left," said Mrs. Jordan.

"Did you see that roan? Isn't he the most beautiful horse you ever saw," Laurie Leigh still had her face pressed against the car window trying to still see the horses. But, they were well past the horse farm.

"We're here. Now, let's see if I can find a place to park," Mr. Jordan said. He found a place on a side street. After he parked the car the family walked to join the crowd in front of the courthouse.

The streets were decorated with flags on every light pole. Red, white and blue swags were hanging from the storefronts and vendors were selling balloons, fireworks, peanuts and lemonade. At the end of Main Street a platform was set up for the town dignitaries to make speeches.

Soon the sound of bands playing filled the air. Toby and Laurie Leigh ran to the curb to get a good place to watch. The local high school band led the parade, followed by patriotic floats depicting scenes from American history. First was the county historic society's "Washington Crossing the Delaware." June McDonald, Seafood Queen, waved her white-gloved hand to the crowd as her daddy drove a brand new red convertible from his downtown car sales lot.

Laurie Leigh waved back and hollered, "Hey Miss June!" June McDonald was her teacher's daughter. Toby and his friend, Bobby, were buying a big pink fluff of cotton candy and hardly paying attention to the parade until the mounted police rode by on their horses.

"Laurie Leigh, here they come," Toby hollered to his sister.

Six uniformed policemen waved to the crowd. The horses walked calmly, not a bit bothered by the noise that occasionally included firecrackers. They'd been trained to be steady in any circumstances.

The last thing in the parade was the town's new fire truck. The whole community had helped pay for the truck with fish fries, rummage sales and raffles. It had taken a whole year. The crowd cheered and the fireman blew the siren. That didn't upset the police horses either.

As the parade disappeared around Palmetto Street the crowd spread out all over town. Some folks headed down to the park to hear the speeches, mostly the grownups. Some wandered into the shops to see what was on sale. Toby and Laurie Lee got in line to buy some sparklers from one of the street vendors.

The brother and sister were just giving the man their money when they heard someone shout, "Look there! Marsh Tackies are coming!"

Laurie Leigh ran back to the curb to look in the direction the lady was pointing who had just shouted. The street was still blocked from traffic because of the parade. Coming right down the middle of the street was a herd of horses being led by one magnificent roan stallion. The sound of their hooves clip clopping on the pavement reminded Laurie Leigh of an old movie she'd watched that had horses trotting down a cobblestone path.

Soon the crowd was lining the street again to watch this second parade. The horses pranced their way to the park, then stopped and began grazing in the grass around the platform. Of course the excitement interrupted the mayor just as he was beginning his speech.

Toby laughed and pointed toward the road at a man running behind the little horses. He had a halter and leadrope in his hand. "How's he going to catch that bunch of horses with one halter?" Toby asked.

But Laurie Leigh recognized the roan horse at the front of the group. It was the herd sire from the farm they had passed on the way to the parade. She knew if the roan was caught the mares would follow him back home.

"That's odd. "Boomer" is usually kept in a stall except when he's turned out for exercise. How did Boomer get loose? And all those mares?" Laurie

Leigh was talking to herself. By then most of the men were heading the horses back the way they'd come.

"Stop, stop!" the man with the halter called, "Everyone just be still and let them settle down."

The men waited and the horses started grazing again. The farm manager, the man with the halter, walked slowly toward Boomer. Boomer raised his head and watched the man. Just as he was close enough to reach out toward the horse and hopefully slip the halter over his head Boomer turned tail and trotted away. Then the mares began to trot and the men began to run after them.

Laurie Leigh and Toby laughed, but then Laurie Leigh got worried. What if a car was coming and didn't see the horses in time. She and her brother followed the crowd to the edge of town. The horses were running right down the road toward the farm.

"Well, that's a relief. It looks like they are going home," Mr. Jordan said, "There, Mr. Raines has caught the roan. I suspect the mares will follow him back."

"I guess they just wanted to be in the parade,"

Laurie Leigh said.

The Jordans walked back to their car and drove to the beach to swim and have their picnic, but Toby and Laurie Leigh couldn't stop thinking about the Marsh Tackies who had come to the parade to celebrate Independence Day.

Chapter Fifteen
A Brief History of South Carolina's Marsh Tackies

Marsh Tackies are small, hardly horses that are also descended from the horses brought to the New World by European explorers. They adapted to the harsh coastal conditions, survived hurricanes and thrived during the hot summers. A few wild herds remain in coastal South Carolina but most are now domesticated and live on farms of a few dedicated breeders who believe the horses are an important part of South Carolina's heritage.

During the American Revolution, Marsh Tackies were used by the colonial militia and the famous "Swamp Fox," General Francis Marion, because they were so well adapted to the marshes and swamps of South Carolina's Low Country. This aided the militia to best the British troops whose English horses could not travel well in that terrain.

They were also used as calvary mounts by Confederate soilders during the Civil War and by the Mounted Beach Patrol during World War II.

Today they are favorite mounts for wild hog

hunting because of their ability to go through the rough terrain of the South Carolina coastal region.

In 2010 the state of South Carolina named the Marsh Tacky as the state's official Heritage Horse.

Glossary

American Quarter Horse – A breed developed in America by crossing horses imported from England and the Colonial Spanish Mustangs. They are known for agility and speed over short distances.

American Revolution – The war for independence between the American colonists and England in the 1700s.

Apparatus – Materials designed for a particular use.

Banker Pony – A term for the wild horses that live on the Outer Banks, which is where the name "Banker" originated. They are also called Spanish Colonial Mustangs and Marsh Tackies.

Barrier Island – A long island lying parallel to the mainland created by the wind and waves building up the sand over many years. It protects the mainland from the action of the ocean.

Brackish – Salty

Cargo – merchandise or goods carried in a ship.

Cattle guard – a bridge-like device that is built over a canal or creek so people can drive over. It has a grid or spaces that cows will not walk across. It saves time, since a gate is not needed.

Chisholm Trail – A cattle trail used by cowboys in the 1800s to move cattle from Texas to Kansas.

Climatic changes – Changes in the patterns of weather over a long period of time.

Colt – a young male horse, under two years old.

Commodity – something useful to market for a profit.

Contagious – A disease that can be spread by contact from one person or animal to another.

Crossbred – The offspring of two different breeds of horses.

Dam – The mother of a horse.

Debris – Trash or the remains of something broken. For example: leaves and branches torn from a tree in a storm.

Developer – A person who plans and builds commercial and residential areas like shopping centers and apartments.

Domesticated – An animal that has been raised in human contact for work, food, transportation, or companionship.

Dredging operation – Digging out a waterway to

make it deeper.

EIA – Equine Infectious Anemia, a disease transmitted to horses by biting insects. There is no cure.

Equine – horse.

Equestrian – A person skilled in the art of riding horseback.

Estuarine– Things that live in and around a water passage where the tide meets the river current.

Euthanize – To kill a hopelessly sick or injured animal in a quick and painless way to relieve suffering.

Feral – An animal that was once domestic, but has since become wild.

Ferry boat – A boat used to carry people and/or vehicles from one place to another when there is no bridge.

Filly – a young female horse, under two years old.

First mate – The person on a ship who is second in command to the captain.

Foal – A baby horse.

Foam – A mass of tiny bubbles that form in top of

the waves.

Freeze brand – A type of brand that permanently marks the horse and causes less pain than hot branding. A super cold iron is used, which alters the pigment in the hair causing it to turn white.

Gelded – A male horse that has been castrated (the testicles removed).

General William Skinner – The commander of a Patriot militia in Perquimans County, North Carolina during the American Revolution.

Genetic – Trelated to the study of heredity.

Graveyard of the Atlantic – The name given the coastal waters off Cape Hatteras because of over 600 ship wrecks that have occurred in that area.

Great Dismal Swamp – A huge and ancient swampland that covers over 100,000 acres in southeastern Virginia and northeastern North Carolina. It is home to a variety of mammals including deer, bear, bobcats and otters, over 50 species of reptiles and turtles, and 200 species of birds. It is a National Wildlife Refuge.

Hands – A horse is measured in hands, which equal

four inches, from the ground to the top of its shoulder (withers.)

Harem – A group of mares that are controlled by a stallion.

Heritage – Tradition and history handed down from generation to generation.

Hull – The frame or body of a ship.

Hurricane – A tropical storm with winds reaching 74 miles per hours or more.

Kayak – A boat first made by Eskimos. It is built on a frame, and the Eskimos covered it with skins. Today fiberglass or other man-made materials are used. The person sits in the middle and paddles with a double-edged paddle.

Legend – A widely accepted, but unproven, story.

Lord Dunmore – The Royal Governor of Virginia in the 1700s. He led the British in the battle of Great Bridge, where the Patriots defeated him.

Land Pirate – Pirates who worked by staying on land and luring ships to shore, then robbed them of their cargo.

Mare – An adult female horse.

Maritime Forest – A forest near the sea.

Marsh Tacky – A name for the wild horses of the Carolina coast. They were called this because of their ability to survive on a diet of marsh grass. Wild horses in South Carolina and Georgia are still called Marsh Tackies today.

Midwife – A person who helps the mother deliver her baby.

Militia – An army that forms for a specific duty then disbands afterward.

Mustang – A horse descended from the Spanish horses brought to America by explorers in the 1500s. Many of North Carolina's wild horses have been registered in the Spanish Mustang Registry.

Nullified – To make powerless or take away legal force.

Oyster shell path – a path paved with oyster shells. Driveways and paths made from these shells are common in coastal Carolina.

Paddock – An enclosed area where a horse can exercise.

Patriots – The American colonists.

Pedigree – The chart that shows an animal's descendents.

Phenomenon – An unusual or rare event.

Pony – A small horse, under 58 inches.

Pony Penning – An event where the wild ponies are rounded up and driven into pens.

Porpoise – A small species of whale.

Public Domain – Land that belongs to the public.

Quarantined – To be kept out of contact with others, usually to prevent a disease from spreading.

Sand bar – A ridge, or hill of sand in a body of water.

Sight board – A board nailed to the top of a wire fence. It reinforces the fence and makes it easier for the animals to see.

Slicker – Rain gear, a long raincoat made of fabric coated with a slick substance like oil.

Shoal – Shallow waters.

Starboard – The rights side of a ship.

Superintendent – A person in charge.

Surfman – The person who patrolled the beach.

Thoroughbred – A breed that originated in England, known for its speed and stamina. They are best known as racehorses.

Vice – A bad habit.

Yearling – A horse that is one year old.

Yellow fever – A tropical disease spread to humans by the bite of an infected mosquito.

Resources

Corolla Wild Horse Fund

http://www.corollawildhorses.com/

1129 Corolla Village Road

Corolla, NC 27927

252-453-8002

Fort Raleigh National Historic Site

Rt 1, Box 675, Manteo, NC 27954

252-473-5773

Foundation for Shackleford Horses

shackhorsemail@gmail.com

306 Golden Farm Road, Beaufort, NC 28516

919-780-8430

Frisco Native American Museum

PO Box 399, Frisco, NC 27936

252-993-4440

Lost Colony Outdoor Drama

Waterside Theare, Fort Raleigh National Historic

Site (June-August) 252-473-3414

Marsh Tackie Association -

http://www.marshtacky.org/

Roanoke Island Festival Park

http://roanokeisland.com/

1 Festival Park, Manteo, NC 27954

252-475-1500

About Donna Campbell Smith

Donna Campbell Smith worked in the horse industry as an instructor, breeder, and trainer for over thirty years. Retired from teaching and training, she now works as an author, freelance writer, and photographer from her home near Raleigh, North Carolina.

In addition to her children's novels, *Pale as the Moon, Bear Song,* and *An Independent Spirit,* Donna has four non-fiction books published by The Lyons Press: *The Book of Miniature Horses, The Book of Draft Horses, The Book of Mules,* and *The Book of Donkeys.* Her work has appeared in many print and online publications.

Donna Campbell Smith has an AAS Degree in Equine Technology from Martin Community College. She is a certified riding instructor and served many years as a Master NC 4-H Horse Program Volunteer. She is a member of Franklin County Arts Council.

CPSIA information can be obtained
at www.ICGtesting.com
Printed in the USA
LVHW082248180819
628092LV00015B/1224/P